HOW

THE GUN RIGHTS DEBATE

HOW TO WIN IT

Tarl Warwick
2023

COPYRIGHT AND DISCLAIMER

All rights reserved. No part of this publication may be reproduced, distributed, or transmitted in any form or by any means, including photocopying, recording, or other electronic or mechanical methods, without the prior written permission of the publisher, except in the case of brief quotations embodied in critical reviews and certain other noncommercial uses permitted by copyright law.

In no way may this text be construed as condoning or encouraging any violent or illegal act. In no way does the author encourage or condone any violent or illegal act. All action is the responsibility of the reader.

FOREWORD

This little work is meant as a primer for those who, like myself, hold the second amendment of the US constitution as important and inalienable. Attendant to the basic premise are several simple subjugate components; the right to keep (own) and bear (carry and use) arms- which is not limited to firearms, per se, although that tends to be the central debate. Some attempts (successful and unsuccessful) have been made by those who hate the idea of the militia, to even "regulate" (in the modern, not original, sense of the term!) or outright ban even things as innocuous as body armor- which after all is not a weapon but a defensive mechanism against weapons.

Here, I hope to elucidate some common arguments and counter-arguments made on the debate in general (one which patriotic militia would never deem necessary to have, but which we are unfortunately compelled to) and attempt to do two things.

First, to categorize the arguments and counterarguments as ineffective or effective. Some points on the subject are simply better than others. If such a public debate is to be won it is required that proponents of the right to bear arms- and attendant subjugate rights- make satisfactory arguments on that token; that the arguments and their premises are strong, and that the counter-arguments to the same made by those who stupidly reject the rights of the militia at large be more easily debased.

Secondly, to examine, similarly, arguments and counter-arguments made by those who do oppose said right to bear arms, and suggest reasoned responses, based on historical accuracy, effectiveness in general, and other considerations.

Hail Columbia.

THE ARGUMENTS

Within the context of the following sections, I will explain the basic arguments generally made, and where possible, provide my analysis of their effectiveness. In some cases, counterarguments will also be discussed.

I: EXAMPLES OF WEAPONS TECHNOLOGY

There are some good arguments to be made here; the Founding Fathers of course realized that weapons technology was not limited to muskets, swords, and smoothbore cannons. They also realized that weapons technology would continue to advance, and never made a mention of finding this problematic. We will later discuss this omission as relevant to the debate over the right to keep and bear arms.

First I would like to give a few examples of *weak* arguments in favor of gun ownership based on issues with the weapons themselves as referred to. There are four of them which are mentioned most frequently: The Puckle Gun, early (even 16th century) revolving pistols, the Kalthoff rifle, and the Girardoni air rifle. Before I elaborate on *why* these are weak examples in favor of a more expansive and well regulated (armed and trained) militia, I will briefly mention that I do actually comprehend the premise of the arguments made; the point may be accurate and proper, but it is still, nonetheless, a weak one- as mostly these weapons are framed in the context of being examples of "semiautomatic weapons", therefore used predominantly to explain why more modern semiautomatic rifles should be readily available to the militia. Again; I sympathize with the *premise*, but I warn that the *examples* are the weak point. I shall explain further and then provide a context in which these examples are considerably stronger.

The Puckle Gun, developed in the early 1700s, is a weak example when used to defend the right of the militia to bear modern weaponry. The particular design is that of a revolving deck gun on a tripod- it was a formidable weapon, and certainly held considerable advantages over the front-loaded deck guns of the age.

However, the operation is manual (not semiautomatic) having to be manually cranked after each shot is fired. As we will see with early revolver technology, this single-action usage is not even relevant to any debate about genuinely semiautomatic weapons. The increased rate of fire has more to do with the revolver being able to hold multiple rounds, and nothing to do with the cycling action. It should also be noted that the weapon never seems to have actually been used for any purpose whether by a standing army or a citizen militia, and the technology was, amusingly, entirely outdated by the time the constitution was penned.

A few examples of revolvers dating to as early as the mid 16th century exist. They were almost never utilized because of the expense involved with smithing such a weapon. They were single action- in fact it wouldn't be until the middle of the 19th century that any double-action revolvers (which could be construed as semi-automatic weapons) were invented. Again, when utilized *specifically* as a defense for the ownership of modern weapons- which are almost always semi-automatic, the early revolver serves no purpose.

The Kalthoff repeating rifle is a bit better as an example- they were actually used in military service, held the powder and ball internally, and so forth. Nonetheless, these repeating rifles, while sophisticated well beyond muskets, were not adopted widely, because of the fouling of their mechanisms and the cost involved with production. As before, these were *not* semi-automatic, they were lever action. However, there is one very positive argument in favor of gun rights to be made based on this particular basic design premise- over the course of a century from invention in the mid 17th century, through the end of their general course of use, multiple offshoots of the same type of weapon displayed greater and greater properties- such as larger capacity, different systems for the loading process, and better reliability. The founders would not only have been aware of such weapons, they would have considered even a reasonably advanced lever action system (and its attendant far higher rate of fire than any musket of the era) to be outdated!

The Girardoni air rifle is the only genuinely semi-automatic example I see used which relates to the debate. It was used in military service and in government service (including in the famed Lewis and Clark expedition), was reliable, and held advantages over the musket. However, this weapon was pneumatic- it has more in common with some air rifles sold today (which are better than the Girardoni!) than it does with an AR-15 or AK-47. As with the Kalthoff, there is a better argument to be made with regards to this weapon; namely that it held a detachable magazine with a 20 shot capacity... the Founders were aware of the ability of this technology to be used, and apparently did not consider what some deem a "high capacity" magazine to be problematic.

Altogether these weapons serve better in an argument over the Founders' recognizing that weapons technology would advance. The omission of any negative feelings about this on their behalf is a much better premise and far more effective than (falsely) claiming that they were semi-automatic in form and function (other than the pneumatic Girardoni.) In short *the founders were aware that weapon technology would advance, supported such advancement, and never said one mumbling word about this being a problem*.

II: THE DEFINITION OF AN "ASSAULT RIFLE"

What is an assault rifle? Do they even exist? This particular line of debate is always at risk of stretching out endlessly and being bogged down in nuance and differential definitions, thus causing all participants in the conversation getting lost in the weeds and underbrush. As such, I consider nitpicking nuance on the subject to be largely useless.

"Assault rifle" effectively has *two* working definitions, which means that debate over the usage is meaningless.

First, we must study the actual proper definition; it means, simply, a select fire weapon, capable of both semi-automatic, and automatic, fire. We might think of an M16- a military weapon widely used by numerous militaries because of its reliability, relatively cheap manufacture, and modular capabilities. The AK47 (at least military variants) is another example and has similar capabilities. It should be noted that the debate between which of these two weapons is "better", according to gun owners, is another bog-down distraction.

Second, there is the *colloquial* usage. In this usage, an assault rifle is any rifle which is semi-automatic and has a military aesthetic, or "enhancements" which "improve" its functionality- a pistol grip, a "high" (standard) capacity magazine, a suppressor, etc.

The argument itself is useless for both those who support expansive gun rights and those who oppose them, because there is no unified definition- the proponent of gun rights will discard the colloquial usage, and the adversary of gun rights will discard the proper but older definition. As such, this particular argument should be avoided in all usage, *even if the argument is technically apt*, because it is without purpose.

III: LIES, DAMN LIES, AND STATISTICS

I personally consider crime statistics *mostly* irrelevant for one very important reason; they have absolutely nothing to do with the constitutional debate over the function of the militia, the meaning of arms, and so forth. In addition, the old adage "there are lies, damn lies, and statistics" bears mentioning. Artificially selecting data often allows for arguments to be made which would not otherwise be feasible- debating the subject, therefore, is more a cat-and-mouse game of data limitation than anything meaningful; shall we debate the rate of gun homicide? Gun deaths? Unjustifiable gun deaths? Mass shootings? Gun deaths by type of weapon- of course artificially categorized by bureaucrats? We can easily compile these numbers and, with proper analysis, arrive at a half a dozen conclusions all over the board; guns are evil, guns are good, guns are situationally useful. Statistics are almost always presented to beguile, not to inform.

There is one particular element of statistics involving guns and the United States that is pertinent- and that is the clear and objective fact that- save for suicide rates unconnected to gun ownership (for other methods of suicide are also disproportionate in such cases)- the rate of deaths attributed to firearms in the United States which did not involve justifiable reasons (self defense, namely), the United States is- outside of a few large metropolitan areas- as safe as areas in nations with considerably more stringent laws regarding firearm ownership.

I personally tend to dovetail this basic fact with an observation that most firearm related deaths that do not take place as part of a state-actor war or conflict, tend to correlate with ethnic cleansings and other such nasty subjects and take place in nations where government bodies severely restrict firearm ownership, such as China, Venezuela, Somalia, etc. This is normally countered by those who despise the right to bear arms, by pointing out that these nations are not developed ones. The subsequent counter is simple; they are claiming that the destitute are more inclined to violence than people with more means- something which does not translate to US gun crime data unless you fix for the obvious; namely, gang activity in cities which is often related to drugs, and almost always involves concealable handguns.

This latter point is technically irrelevant; the ability to conceal a weapon has now effectively become a dead issue entirely and it is nigh on self evident that the founders intended people to carry arms however they wished, concealed or otherwise. Indeed, some states *required* the carrying of firearms- at least for male citizens- for quite some time.

In some cases I see racial crime statistics being utilized by those promoting the general welfare by supporting the right of the militia to own and carry weapons. This is unhelpful at best and asinine at worst- a handful of inner city gang members and thugs will never speak for the vast corpus of the US population, which is peace-loving and wishes in many cases to maintain that peace by making sure that victimizing citizens is too risky a practice to engage in. Such statistics are no different from others- which is to say, easily misinterpreted. If we arbitrarily define what is urban or rural, we can also see a vast divide on the same issue. We can also fix for gender- women are massively less likely to kill someone with a firearm than are males- but this is a pointless meandering that all too many people engage in; it is at once unhelpful, and statistically spurious.

IV: NONE OF THE FOUNDERS COMPLAINED ABOUT WEAPONS TECHNOLOGY ADVANCING

Partially as a takeoff of my prior discussion in section I, I wanted to point out one particularly pertinent argument with regards to gun rights- namely, that the founders saw a number of technological advances in military arms both during their lives generally, and after the Revolutionary War which they fought.

And despite this, they never said one thing to the effect that this was problematic, or caused them alarm. Not a single founder (indeed as far as I know not a single *human being*) in the United States for the first half of the 19th century, ever uttered a word regarding this topic. While the last "true" founder (Madison) died in 1836, the last (proven) soldier to fight in the Revolution did not die until 1868 (John Gray.) Despite having seen the development of the *Mine ball*, (sometimes misallocated as the "miniball") and other advancements of the era, surviving members of the original militia are, to my knowledge, entirely absent in having supported any form of curb on the ability of private citizens to own any form of weapon in the age, not just the founders.

This omission is a relevant one. What is not particularly relevant are quotes from the founders and others from the late 1700s in *support* of the militia- at least those outside of the Federalist Papers and similar accredited accounts of their opinions. Why do I make this distinction? Because the modern square of debate over this and every other issue tends to be a digital one, and many quotes are fabricated or at least unattributed. For example, many readers will likely have heard the quote "The strongest reason for the people to retain the right to keep and bear arms is, as a last resort, to protect themselves against tyranny in government." This comes from Thomas Jefferson, does it not? Although I am sure he would have agreed with the basic premise of the quote, it does not actually come from Jefferson, or even a contemporary time period.

There are numerous examples of this issue; in some cases, quotes are accurate but attributed incorrectly, especially some quotes from several individuals in the drafts of the Virginia constitution- while these are therefore not discredited, they are still *weak* arguments against antigunnery, because the antigunner will (if they know the pedigree of the quote(s)) simply point out that the draft language "did not reflect the final views of the signees." This is nonsense of course, but it is still a counter to the argument- an argument in which of course one is not attempting to convert the bona fide hater of the militia, but rather any onlooker whose intellectual merit is great enough for their mind to be changed.

I do not argue that quotes from the founders or from other people are irrelevant; on the contrary they can be of great import- but the pedigree of such quotations should be established before they are employed in an argumentative manner. I strongly suggest the reading of the Federalist Papers to all who seek to use this particular facet of United States history as a debating point. What is, at least in my opinion, of greater import than any singular opinion, is rather the *lack* of any opinion against the private ownership of firearms, including those developed for the decades after the Revolution.

V: "TWO ROUNDS A MINUTE!"

This particular claim is one made by those who dislike the second amendment and is debunked entirely. What remains is to detail the specific arguments nullifying its effectiveness.

The claim involves muskets- the admittedly most common form of weapon available in the late 18th century. The extension of this is the claim (which isn't even true) that muskets could fire "only two rounds every minute" and that the founders therefore would be horrified by modern weapons.

We will discuss some of the minutiae of this argument in a further section regarding weapon originalism, but the premise itself is completely false; a trained musketeer could achieve at least three and often four shots in a minute, and specifically elite veterans could unload a fifth.

I point this out for accuracy's sake; but the argument is needless; five shots in a minute is still far short of anything achieved by a single action revolver, let alone a modern firearm. The counter-argument is therefore *weak* and will of necessity lead to a counter to the counter-argument involving the firing rate of actual modern weapons.

It is the inaccuracy of the claim which should be targeted- without this further, needless elaboration. It would be far more effective to mention the Kalthoff rifle and other weapons in the era which could fire eight or more balls in short order without any need to reload.

VI: RECREATIONAL MCNUKES

One hyperbolic talking point I have witnessed in use is *normally* meant to be facetious- either to bother those who dislike the right to bear arms, or to jokingly show dedication to the Second Amendment; the basic foil is the suggestion that civilians ought to own nuclear weapons.

However, this premise is also used (in literal or near-literal) form by people who seriously consider this to be a good and constitutional idea. I recognize that I am only speaking about a minority of people who ever invoke "recreational nukes" but it bears mentioning that the argument is not simply a weak one, but not a constitutional one at all, when we understand the meaning of the militia (and of regulation and arms, which we will define more amply in a later section.)

The militia (effectively the body of citizens at large) has the inalienable right to own and carry weapons. The explicit purpose of this right is multifaceted- the most important provision being the protection of the United States itself from adversaries foreign or domestic, ostensibly in a defensive manner on domestic soil, as the founders did not envision engaging in foreign wars in the manner of Europe- we can understand this after a brief perusal of quotations from their papers and books (at least those we can vouch for as authentic- again with those spurious quotes!)

Can a nuclear weapon be effectively used on domestic soil for the purposes of defending ones' nation? In a situational manner, perhaps, but in general, the notion is not a practical one, for reasons which should be fairly obvious; a nuclear weapon is not discriminate in who dies within the blast radius- deploying one even on, say, a city or area overrun with enemy forces (foreign or domestic) would also kill thousands or even millions of citizens. The idea, in a nutshell, is insane.

There is, however, a *strong* argument derived from the patently humorous notion of recreational nuclear weapons; when the argument is made (seriously or facetiously) the resulting reaction from those who dislike the right to bear arms is normally that of confusion and incredulity, whether they understand it to be a joke or not. Yet these same individuals occasionally trot out the argument that the right to bear arms has been nullified *because the US government possesses similar weapons systems*; it runs, basically; "your rifle is meaningless. Uncle Sam has tanks and fighter jets and nukes."

How very odd! The suggestion of domestic usage of nuclear weapons in the context of the militia is considered laughable, or insane, yet the same suggestion is made regarding the government itself! This same benevolent government, I note, is the one they would entrust to disarm the militia.

Again we admit that the notion is not promoted by the majority of those who dislike the notion of a well functioning militia or civilian body which is armed- as with the suggestion of civilian nuclear weapons, the argument is only made by a few hard-liners, and people who are attempting to deliberately antagonize.

It should be noted that a well regulated (properly functioning) militia has no way to field nuclear weapons- the militia comprising *individual components* (singular people) who must bear their own arms, first, and second, in the *organized capacity*- which allows for armories, training ranges, etc. But it is not conceivable that even a fairly well organized paramilitary group would be able to develop, maintain, and properly use a nuclear weapon. The argument is normally a funny joke, but some militia do not seem to comprehend how a militia regulating itself would be unable to do so if it were attempting to field nuclear weapons, and why the usage is asinine in the context of domestic defense of self, property, family, community, or nation.

VII: ANTIGUNNERS FALSE ORIGINALISM

Those who do not support the inherent rights of the militia often resort to one particular argument, almost more than all of the others- a sort of *faux originalism*, in which it is claimed that gun control (at least as lucratively marketed by its advocates) does not seek to disarm the militia, or any member thereof, but merely seeks to ban, highly regulate, or highly tax, certain classes of weapons- notably rifles of a semi-automatic nature which they have arbitrarily condemned as "assault weapons"- that term we have already spoken of. The argument effectively states that particular weapons manufactured relatively recently are more pernicious than others, and therefore would not have been countenanced by the founders, or that the constitution does not protect them because they are modern, and did not exist in the late 18th century.

The argument is at once disingenuous and easily discredited. We may approach the premise from multiple angles.

First, as we have already noted, the founders were aware of advances in weapons technology during their lifetimes and those in relatively recent history- the latter, since many of them were apparently versed in history and military affairs. They knew of weapons which were, in that time period, novel, and said nothing to the effect of that being an issue. The concept that they "could not have known weapons would fire so quickly" or something to that basic effect is a moot point; nobody can ask the founders their opinion of weapons from the last fifty years or so and get them to voice their opinions- since this is the case, it can just as easily (and likely more accurately) be claimed that every one of them would be clamoring to buy a modern semi-automatic rifle, and probably considerably more ammunition than many modern gun owners own.

Second, we have the rabbit hole, the slippery slope, of this originalism. While the founders understood that revolvers, lever action rifles, and at least pneumatic semi-automatic weaponry existed, they did not understand that semi-automatic weapons would exist in the form they do today. The antigunner is fundamentally right when they make this claim; however, the founders also did not know that self contained cartridges (that is, a bullet with the primer, powder, and casing, all as one) would exist. They did not know about polymers. They did not have access to any double action revolver. They did not comprehend that cannons could be breech-loaded- a technology already in use in the 19th century, long before the present. The slippery slope here is that of accepting the premise proffered by the opponent of the militia- to allow the banning of modern rifles, and similar weapons, would also allow the banning of effectively any weapon with a technological advancement beyond that of the mid 19th century at latest, rendering virtually all modern arms illegal and rendering the militia both deficient (poorly regulated) and useless as a very concept.

Third, we must consider crime statistics in a dovetailed manner. The founders, it is argued, would have hanged their heads in shame at the rate of death associated with modern weapons, argue the advocates of laws against guns. I argue simply that they would not do so- they would have noted the legions killed by the enemies of the militia and preferred a few sad and unfortunate but inescapable casualties to a much larger number imparted by a foreign army, domestic tyrant, or other malevolent force. Notably, the types of weapons specifically targeted by those who despise the militia tend to be used in a tiny minority of gun crimes, let alone out and out homicides- and the founders, if we conceive of them as wise, would spend a few days pondering the situation and prefer to simply begin executing inner city gang members when they are caught, thus solving a large bulk of the problem.

The fourth point countering this faux originalism is

perhaps the strongest; the same logic (or lack thereof) is not in any way applied to other elements of the constitution. The right to free speech extends to digital communication, not just papers written via fountain pen. The tenth amendment and its enshrining of the rights of states extends to states beyond the first thirteen colonies which became states originally as of the ratification of the US constitution. The right to privacy extends beyond simply ones' home- it is understood to extend to ones' automobile (something the founders never envisioned) and so forth. The right to a fair trial has not been nullified by demographic changes, or changes in the composition of citizens available in trials- namely, with the extension of full legal citizenship to, say, women, or black individuals, initially freed slaves.

The founders did not live in a time in which women were members of the militia, or in which communication was mostly predicated upon the usage of monopolized digital platforms. Nonetheless, no similar argument is ever made in an attempt to denigrate *any* other right other than the right to keep and bear arms- a telling attempt at subjugation, sometimes out of malice, sometimes ignorance, and sometimes fear.

VIII: WHAT IS REGULATION? WHAT IS THE MILITIA?

Linguistics play a role in the debate over gun rights; those who dislike the concept of a broadly armed civilian militia often point to the wording of the Second Amendment and claim that it protects only the right of a state or national guard to bear arms, or that the civilian militia must be regulated by the government; an open-ended proposal which, of course, would allow effectively any regulation it decided to administer.

The claim is false. And this particular argument is *strong*. We know that "militia" cannot refer to state administered guard (or a military) because no such institution of the former existed at the time the US constitution was written, and the latter would have been labeled "regulars" or "soldiers." To "do soldiering" was a paid and state administered concept- the militia were merely civilians who happened to own arms and were willing to muster as necessary. Their arms did not get stored in an armory when mustering was not in effect. In a few states, it was even commanded that civilians carry weapons in some situations- clearly, not as part of an organized (or even disorganized) militia.

In the parlance of the late 18th century, militia has literally only one meaning; "all able-bodied citizens eligible by law to be called on to provide military service supplementary to the regular armed forces." This expansive term originally intended only male and white citizens, but has since broadened considerably. Importantly, the fact that a civilian militia can be called upon as such, does *not negate* their own personal ownership of arms, as was the case for the entire militia in the United States for a protracted period of time. These arms had to essentially match those of regular troops (soldiers) because otherwise the militia was meaningless and useless. The militia is comprised of every citizen who has attained the age of majority (now the age of 18) and who is not incarcerated, crippled, or a criminal lunatic.

"Regulation" requires some elaboration. The usual parlance in which the term is employed nowadays is that of government regulation; but as we will see, that concept is actually a *linguistic subjugate* to regulation at large, which does not require a government, or even any organized entity. This point is, also, I propose, a *strong* one, eliminating one of the core debating points of those who seek to undermine our militia.

The definition of "regulate" in Cambridge is as follows: "to control something, especially by making it work in a particular way." Does this require government intervention? Of course not. The term was used usually in a mechanical context in the late 18th century- a watch was regulated by being properly wound, and a diet was regulated by being neither excessive nor deficient. The concept of regulation as a government-down aspect of society really seems to come about in the United States around the end of the 19th century, when rules established by the government "supposedly" to help order society became more frequent.

But the term is subjugate. "Government regulation" is a component of "regulation" in the same way that "Tropical fruit" is a subjugate of "fruit." This basic premise is easy to understand.

There is one final point, and an *important* one to make here: The militia could not even refer to regular soldiers because none existed at the time to refer to. Regulation clearly refers to personal and group regulation in the context of the Second Amendment, and cannot refer to federal government regulation, as *none existed until the Cruikshank decision in the 1870s long after the founders had died.*

IX: GUN CRIME AND GANGS

One strong and pertinent point in favor of gun rights is simply a nullification of one layer of the argument made by those who seek to further restrict the militia- namely that most gun crime in the United States (that is usages of firearms not related to self harm, accidents, or defensive AKA justified usage) involve handguns, gangs, and inner cities. Yes, indeed, a significant majority involve only a small number of very large metropolitan areas, often run politically by people who at least in public statements are fairly averse to the rights of the militia.

This is often countered by several examples of cities with high gun crime rates being relatively near to states where gun laws are very relaxed- a prime example is the extremely crime-ridden Chicago, not far from the border of Indiana. It suffices to point out that the availability of firearms in Indiana does not seem to have caused the state itself a high rate of gun crimes- at least outside of a few large urban areas such as Indianapolis. The correlation between urban areas and gun crime is substantial- and it almost always involves weapons which are not even targeted by those who argue against the supremacy of the second amendment, not the "scary" weapons they typically target.

Even a large portion of "mass shootings" (a label which was changed years ago to include substantially more shootings, by redefining how may victims needed to exist for the label to apply- another statistical obfuscation!) involve gang crimes; especially drive-by shootings and revenge killings.

None of these things have anything to do with the activities of a militia, and rarely involve perpetrators outside of said metropolitan zones. Oddly, banning metropolitan cities would arguably reduce gun crime more than any proposed laws against firearms themselves.

X: GUN CRIMES VS GUN DEATHS

Statistical shenanigans!

A common tactic employed by *both* sides of the debate over gun rights, the militia at large, and even self defense in and of itself *even in the absence of the usage of firearms* is the shifting and cherry picking of data related to the use of weapons in crime, or in a defensive manner, or in general, and the convolution is wide and deep- it is employed almost invariably in debates, and should *always* be focused on, because it might be the weakest point brought up by those who despise the rights of the civilian militia. This particular debate plays out over and over again especially in public discourse- far more, these days, than among the self credited "intelligentsia", or researchers, or even the state media, which is the new and proper moniker of what was once simply the state-adjacent corporate press.

Shall we fixate on gun *deaths*? Well, that includes justifiable deaths, in which someone utilized a firearm to defend themselves against an attacker. Yes, the attacker is dead (or perhaps injured- another statistical oddity- depending on the data involved), but the death was justifiable. It would have been justified, usually, regardless of the manner of self defense. What of suicides? A full third of all gun deaths in the United States (give or take a bit depending on the year the data is derived from), and those suicides often would have occurred even if every firearm magically disappeared- a noose, poison, a cliff or bridge, a knife, a toaster and a full bathtub, there are many ways for a person to kill themselves- guns seem to be often employed because the death is quicker than most, and therefore perceived of as less potentially painful- it is odd to see so many people therefore, who use this data as a cudgel against the lawful militia, then also arguing for assisted suicide (which I admit I support in many cases, as the state has no reason or right to force a person to live.)

Shall we fixate on gun *crimes*? Many of them do not involve even the discharge of a weapon. A gun crime may be simply transporting a firearm improperly under state law, or possession of some accessory- say a standard capacity magazine in a state which only allows low capacity magazines. It could involve negligent discharge even on ones' own property, depending on the area the person is residing in at the time.

Shall we fixate on *school shootings*? This data is commonly trotted out- but it again misses any meaningful central point; it is devoid of meaning- a "school shooting" can involve accidental discharge in an adjacent property, or in the parking lot- it does not need to involve death, or even injury, or even property damage. Yet it tends to be all collected together. A school shooting can involve an intoxicated student showing off a century old revolver to their problematic friends in the parking lot after school hours and accidentally firing the weapon. If we employed this methodology for knife crime, we would surely see an explosion of such cases, commensurate with an "epidemic" of knife crime.

So we can see that the usage of such statistical data is not a helpful one. Normally, when it is compiled at all, it is compiled with a clear-cut bias in one way or the other- to either provide an argument against gun ownership, or in its favor. I believe that using such statistical data in favor of the rights of the militia to be generally on the weak side; but recognizing the data is flawed, pointing this out, and using that basic premise to negate the claims of those who dislike personal firearm ownership is, rather, in my opinion a *strong* argument. It is all about how the analytic numbers are presented, and thus simply countering one set of flawed data with another works less well than discounting *all* of the data at least of this type, as useless.

XI: ARMED POPULATIONS ARE SAFER

As with statistical shenanigans in general, the (false) claim that armed populations are less safe should be debunked in debates with the forces of antigunnery, and it should be pointed out that death due to firearms in the commission of war, civil war, ethnic cleansing, etc, is rarely referred to- because it outright *proves* that armed populations are less likely to suffer mass casualty events.

A population with more cars will of necessity experience more deaths from car accidents. A population with more firearms will experience more deaths from firearms- but this is half the picture, and perhaps not even half of it. A significant portion of gun *deaths* in the United States are justifiable, accidental, or self inflicted (suicide.) Suicidal people do not need firearms to kill themselves, accidents can happen with any potentially deadly item (and in the case where the death was negligent, of course the person will still be negligent with, say, a bow, a knife, or of course, a vehicle.) Justifiable deaths are not a bad thing- indeed, while it is sad when someone has been killed, if their death has saved anothers' life, I would at least personally label it a good thing- which is of course just my own opinion.

Genocide and ethnic cleansing is entirely absent the debate, which is rather unfortunate- I rarely hear proponents of an armed population and militia bring the subject up- but it is a *strong* argument. Vastly more people are killed even in relative times of peace, by armed authorities, state power, or terrorists, than are ever killed by their fellow citizens, because their fellow citizens are rarely lunatics or particularly violent. Indeed, the enormous number of firearms and their owners in the United States- a nation in which (absent aforementioned gang violence) firearm crimes are *relatively uncommon*- speaks volumes about the peace-loving, crime-averse militia. Exactly as the founders intended and understood.

Antigunners will often resort to the retort that ethnic cleansing, etc, cannot "happen here" in a developed nation. Such has been the eternal optimists' ethos before every great genocide and pogrom. It seems that few people in re-industrializing Germany in the 1930s believed that millions of people were about to die. The mostly disarmed optimistic Chinese communist under Maoism probably did not believe that their government was going to oversee nigh on 30,000,000 deaths between execution and famine. These are only a couple of examples- tinhorns and terrorists freely roam much of the world, killing at a whim, because the populations proximate to them have no effective means of fighting back. Only when something particularly egregious happens do they take to the streets in large enough numbers to have any relative safety even in nonviolent protest, let alone do they have the ability to clip off the shackles of tyranny at large. Their only resort is to appeal to military forces which are typically as lawless and tyrannical as the leaders they seek to depose, leading to endless revolution and counter-revolution, as in Libya, Burma, etc.

When "other developed nations" are mentioned as being less violent (which is not even always the case) a proper retort involves a simple truth; those other nations also have relatively large numbers of privately owned firearms (France, Germany, etc) while other nations which disarm their populations are under near constant turbulence. Switzerland is not, despite common belief, the only nation outside of the United States with a decently advanced militia system. Switzerland is reckoned one of the safest nations in the world, having repeatedly been ignored during large-scale wars in Europe because nobody wished to suffer millions of casualties to attack them. The same protection is given the United States, arguably at an order of magnitude greater a level.

XII: US GUN CONTROL BEGINS WITH JIM CROW AND IS RACIST, THE MILITIA IS NOT BASED ON SLAVERY AS CLAIMED

Sometimes, opponents of the lawful militia claim that the second amendment was enshrined by the founders for the purpose of preventing slave revolts- that this is utterly unfounded and no evidence suggests this was even a consideration is fairly obvious- moreover, that a number of states never enacted slavery to begin with, yet ratified the amendment. Indeed, in the Federalist Papers, the opinions of the original members of the United States are clear; the amendment was meant to prevent the formation of a standing army (which was a failure) and to provide for the common defense of individuals and individuals in groups (which was not a failure.)

Indeed, slavery did play a role, however, in the formation of anti-gun laws in the United States, which only began to be passed in the wake of one very special Supreme Court decision in 1876- namely, US v. Cruikshank. I will not bother to detail the entire case here (the reader can research the topic themselves easily)- the short explanation is that the right to bear arms was converted into a privilege, and that the decision was promulgated by the Ku Klux Klan. The unfortunate majority opinion touched on this, and I quote: "...The second amendment declares that it shall not be infringed, but this, as has been seen, means no more than that it shall not be infringed by Congress."

This unfortunate and treasonous decision was upheld for more than a century, allowing states to violate the second amendment with virtual impunity, by declaring that the second amendment does not even say what it says, all to disarm former slaves so that they could be disarmed and therefore helpless against hooded phantoms with nooses and torches. It is not the militia, but the *anti-militia* that was founded on racism.

This decision was thankfully, lawfully, and rightfully overturned only recently, in the year 2010, with another case, namely McDonald v. Chicago, which declared that the second amendment does protect the individual right to bear arms, that the due process clause of the 14th amendment applied to states and not just the federal government (or congress specifically as listed in Cruikshank), and retroactively improved upon the decision in DC. v. Heller two years prior.

If race or racism are ever brought up in the context of a debate regarding gun rights, it is the duty of every member of the militia to commit these *objective facts* to memory and remind whoever is at hand that it was the forces of antigunnery which expounded their legal opinions in order to disarm former slaves, which had become members of the militia when they were made lawful, voting citizens of the United States- some of which had already served in the Union Army during the Civil War, and wielded firearms in the process of doing so.

The proponents of the militia meanwhile are absolutely blameless; those who opposed the decision (and which were legally and civically correct) understood the ruse, attempting to prevent the sole and only legal decision- one sponsored by the Ku Klux Klan- which *effectively led to all anti-gun laws thereafter passed* by state governments. Prior to Cruikshank, there was effectively *no law regarding firearms in the United States at large* that did not involve territorial law (which we will examine further in the next section) or the disarming of lunatics and the mentally disabled, usually by their families, or by the community at large, out of pragmatism, and often extra-judicially.

XIII: TERRITORIAL GUN LAWS DEBUNKED

Meaningful ordinances regarding firearms did indeed exist prior to the Cruikshank decision. They oddly overlap with a period in United States history reckoned to be one of whisky-guzzlin', darn tootin', rugged outlaws, scamps, thieves, and of course, every other stereotypical “Americana” label from Gunsmoke- namely, the territories of the “wild west.”

Indeed, towns in territorial regions organized themselves more or less as they saw fit. A simple democratic vote- or a vote by a council elected by democratic vote- sometimes even just a decision by the elected sheriff, was enough to compel visitors to leave their guns at the door, so to speak. Firearms could be barred from any saloon, hotel, stable, or anything else, at a whim.

But these were unincorporated territories. The tenth amendment did not, strictly speaking, apply at all. Both before and after Cruikshank, wild west justice often relied upon juries, judges, sheriffs, and so forth, that existed somewhat outside of the stringency of the US legal code entirely. This was necessary, if not always proper; state supremacy does not apply when there is no state.

In an odd twist, those who oppose the militia will simultaneously claim that these rules are a traditional basis for gun control in the United States (in order to bypass the recent Bruen decision) while strangely invoking the visage of the supposedly violent and brutal wild west as a reason why their own proposals should be taken seriously. This is all against the backdrop of historical ignorance; again, in that era, little if any meaningful anti-gunnery existed in any incepted part of the United States- that is, with the exception of former slaves after Cruikshank, no real limitations on firearm ownership existed until well into the 20th century- and yet for the most part (and this is key), actual gun crime not involving suicide or legalized terrorism (a la the Klan) was relatively uncommon. Then, as now, random killings tended to be relegated to the streets of a few large cities such as New York or Philadelphia- the wild west, armed to the teeth outside of a few settled trading posts and towns, was actually *relatively peaceful*. Although the trope of the shootout at high noon was relatively *uncommon*, it also belies a fundamental truth- the settler of the wild west was fairly safe in the wilds, unless they were attacked by an animal (necessitating a firearm for defending themselves) or perhaps by "native" forces (necessitating the same.) Outside of these considerations, they were more likely to be assaulted in some manner in one of the brothel-borne towns or settlements in the frontier lands, where they hilariously may have been disarmed at the time.

Ordinances requiring that guns be left with the sheriff, or that they could not be carried in some areas, or that they not be pre-loaded, are all mentioned by proponents of antigunnery, and they are all *fundamentally meaningless*, because they were never in use in states which existed in the 19th and early 20th centuries. They are indeed *relics of a past era* which no longer exists- the era of the settling of territories which became states. If anything this occasionally utilized argument should be countered with a basic truth; proponents of disarming the militia are relying on long dated, outmoded, boring, ancient legalese which was never even incepted by a state entity at all and relied on the democratic actions of people with elementary school educations.

XIV: JAPANESE INTERNMENT CAMPS

We have previously remarked upon the logical fallacy employed by those who hate the militia, in which they ruminate upon the falsehood that “it” (genocide, etc), “cannot happen here.” But it did, unfortunately. This argument is not necessarily the strongest one which can be made in favor of the right of the people to bear arms, but it is a pertinent and accurate one, and perhaps is of use.

In 1942, the socialist president of the United States, Franklin Roosevelt, began the process of putting certain Americans in concentration camps (wrongfully labeled “internment camps”) based on their ethnic and national origin- some hundreds of thousands of American citizens and lawful residents were placed in horrendous prison-like conditions until the middle of 1946. This heinous act was officially apologized for belatedly in 1988, hilariously by Ronald Reagan.

Those who dislike the concept of an armed militia are at a loss to debate this point. If it is pointed out that they ought to have been armed to better resist socialist tyranny, the antigunner must defend the internment. They then obviously resort to sputtering and ranting about the violence of gun owners, of treason, and oddly stating that those resisting would be killed- which implicates the government, not the militia, as violent- it is grave but amusing, since the only violence done in the whole affair was by the socialist government of the age. It must be noted that Franklin Roosevelt is the modern father of US antigunnery, and a reformed version of his national gun registry became what today is known as the National Firearms Act. Few people seem to know this, and fewer seem to apply this to their debate against the antimilitia.

XV: ANTIGUNNER ORIGINALISM IS NOT PRAGMATIC

The faux originalism of the foes of the rights of the lawful militia, we have already touched upon, but here I wanted to give some examples of further follies with regards to their argument; namely, that the founders *did not intend weapons not available in the late 18th century to fall under the constitutional purview of the second amendment*, or that *weapons of a specifically modern character do not fall under the same*. The latter is easily brushed aside- "modern" is a malleable term which changes all the time. The former requires a few bits of constitutional nuance.

Let us apply this logic to some other amendments.

What of the first amendment? Does it only protect the right to free expression when a fountain pen and paper are used? Does the right to speak freely extend to digital communication or begin and end with yelling on the street corner? Shall the press in its modern form be protected, or does the protection only involve the *literal* printing press- a wooden-framed machine manually ordered?

Does the fourth amendment begin and end with literal papers or does it apply more broadly, to digital communication, and so forth? What of the modern mail system which did not exist in the late 18th century?

Does the fifth amendment include the *Miranda* rule as a subjugate? The ruling involved comes far after the penning of the US constitution- are we to consider that null and void under the faux originalism of the hater of the militia? Does due process apply in the digital era at all? Interesting here is the watering down of the Miranda rule of late- viciously opposed by people whose political leanings often put them at odds with a true reading of the second amendment.

Does the 8th amendment hold supremacy? What defines "unusual" punishments? The founders were familiar with forms of punishment which today would be considered absolutely inhumane- are those punishments acceptable due to originalism?

Does the 9th amendment pertain to states created after the founding of the United States? Does the 10th?

The founders were all dead before the 13th amendment was created, and slavery in the United States was abolished (except for in the case of criminals- which is telling.) Shall we re-institute slavery? By the logic of the originalists, the founders never envisioned an assault rifle. They also never envisioned the citizenship of former slaves. Should one proposition be considered more ponderously obtuse than the other? This ties in with the 14th amendment.

The founders never envisioned or could have envisioned an income tax. Is the 16th amendment void? (I chuckle; for I would support the idea.)

The founders wanted senators elected by state congresses, is the 17th amendment void since it apportions senators by popular vote instead?

The founders never envisioned females voting in elections, and indeed likely would have considered the concept hilarious- does that nullify the 19th amendment?

Although Washington technically established the concept of a two-term presidency (one only ignored by the socialist FDR we previously discussed), the founders never seemed to have had much of an opinion on the issue. Should the 22nd amendment be held nullified because the founders never considered term limits for the president?

The 23rd amendment grants electors to the District of Columbia. This was passed into existence in 1960. Would the founders countenance the concept? Should it be held null and void?

The voting age in the United States was 21 until 1971 with the passage of the 26th amendment lowering it to 18. The founders clearly did not intend for these individuals to vote (oddly, for them to be members of the militia!) Should we raise the age back to 21 in accordance with the faux originalism of the enemies of the militia?

I do not ask these questions for any reason other than to show the stupidity of the fake originalism of the enemies of the militia- *no other amendment* is put to the same originality test, any more than they are put to the same test with regards to pragmatism, supposedly because the bearing of arms is dangerous, and therefore unique. That arms are wielded in offense more often than not by people whipped into frenzy by books or speeches is completely ignored.

XVI: DISARMAMENT IS IMPOSSIBLE

Those who oppose the rights of the militia may be loosely split into two camps; those who "simply want common sense gun reform" and have no issue with most weapons and other arms, and those who harbor fantasies about a disarmed public. That this public would be disarmed by people bearing actual military grade firearms seems to escape them.

I will ignore the former; while the slippery slope argument applies to their argument, I have given, and will give further, counters to their position- it is the latter group which I will briefly address here.

Disarming the US militia is effectively impossible, unless they are stupid enough to largely give up their right to bear arms willingly. Together, the US militia forms the largest, most well armed, and arguably most well trained fighting force in the history of the world- hundreds of millions of guns in over one hundred million hands- not to mention the broad assortment of other militaria they possess- body armor, survival equipment, and skills, as well as some millions of them being combat veterans at any given time.

It would take a force beyond reckoning numbering at least in the tens of millions to disarm them. This pipe dream is dismissed as folly more than anything else; it is hardly worth a point even debating however- most who posit the act are not arguing in good faith and are merely seeking to antagonize others, and do not even believe their own bravado.

XVII: THE MILITIA IS LAW ABIDING

Sometimes, those who hate the militia make a particular argument with such an effective counter that I wonder why almost no proponent of bearing arms seems inclined to make it; the claim is an antagonistic one often made in bad faith- that is that the civilian militia has suffered many abuses of its right to bear arms over time, and has never taken up arms in defense of its rightful civic abilities.

This is meant to demoralize those of us who cherish the ability to keep and bear arms; but I have always found that the end effect is to make me laugh- because the claim is effectively that the militia is *peaceable and law abiding*- indeed, it is so peaceable that it is willing to suffer the most obvious of constitutional violations in avoidance of conflict and combat. This is a *strong* point; it directly undercuts the notion of United States citizens as irrational and violent and thus needing further (government) regulation of their arms and their ability to defend themselves; absent violence conducted by criminals who would act in a violent and criminal manner anyways, there are precious few cases of people motivated by the desire to defend the constitution, or civic structure of the United States, becoming violent in any manner, let alone in the act of using a firearm to harm or kill others.

Indeed, while the militia is currently deficient of proper arms, it conforms exactly to that notion which the founders proposed- it is a peace loving civilian corps, which can muster as needed, and has shown a ponderous reluctance to muster even when under stress. The last time the militia effectively did so, to my knowledge, was in the (entirely peaceful) defense of the Bundy ranch against federal bureaucrats, in 2014, A Nevada case which saw numerous individuals indicted by the government only to be acquitted of all charges. *The militia was legally justified in mustering in that case.*

XVIII: THE AR15 BOGEYMAN

We have already examined the nonsensical premise of the use of "assault weapon" as a term because the proper and colloquial usage are so far apart. Now we come to the bogeyman itself; the AR15.

Numerous false claims are peddled about this one particular weapon (and to an extent the AK-47)- I have personally debated several people publicly on the topic of firearms, and the AR-15 is the most common single weapon mentioned by those who dislike the rights of the militia. I am going to explain how several of their misconceptions can be explained- however, as we will see, bothering to do so is a *weak* argument even when it is a necessary one to have; there is, however, a *strong* argument to be derived from the false claims.

The first claim is that "AR15" stands for "Assault Rifle 15." This is false. The "AR" stands for "Armalite Rifle" and bears the moniker of the company producing the weapon.

The second (and astonishingly inaccurate) claim is that the most common round utilized with the weapon (the 5.56) is capable of causing the human body to explode, or that it is particularly powerful and deadly. The 5.56 is an intermediate-capability round largely chosen over the larger, more powerful .308 because of weight and therefore capacity, and is not, actually, all that powerful at all. In some states, it isn't even legal to hunt deer with the round because of the risk of seriously injuring a deer that nonetheless survives, staggering around for hours and being lost by the hunter, causing unnecessary suffering and a lost kill.

The third, is that the weapon is a military weapon. This is patently false. The M16 rifle is a military weapon and the major (and highly significant) difference between the military-issued

M16 and the AR15 civilian rifle is the capability in the former of select fire- that is, to fire a burst of three rounds, or automatic fire, not simply in a semi-automatic manner.

The first argument is weak because nobody cares what the moniker stands for. The argument is made as a mere distraction by opponents of the lawful militia.

The second is weak because the AR platform is highly modular, other weapons chamber 5.56 rounds, and the 5.56 does, admittedly, have a significant chance to considerably injure or kill a human shot with it out of a rifle. Dickering over the round compared to a more powerful round is not going to convince the enemy of the militia (who typically won't understand bullets anyways) to change their mind.

The third is pointless and weak since the militia was meant to bear military grade arms. Indeed, the lack of modern select-fire weapons to the militia is actually a breach of its proper regulation- a point which will cause some to roll their eyes but is clearly both constitutionally and civically proper.

The stronger argument is to briefly mention these claims, debunk them, and merely point out that the person vilifying the weapon is clueless about it, and therefore what they state cannot be counted for as meaningful- if they do not know what the weapon is for, how its ammunition operates, and its origin and terminology, they are showing that they are a *deficiently regulated militia member* and their opinion is thereby useless.

XIX: STOP ASSUMING ALL "GUN CONTROL" ADVOCATES ARE TRYING TO BE EVIL

One exceptionally weak argument sometimes made by well-meaning proponents of the lawful militia is merely an assumption; the assumption of bad faith or malevolence on the part of those who do not agree with the militia being properly armed. A conversation having been enjoined, the supporter of the right to bear arms eventually tires of fallacies and easily debunked talking points, and declares that their opponent is merely "trying to disarm everyone" or "working for some subversive power" or something to that extent.

In my own meanderings into this debate I have encountered some people who declare their opposition to the rights of the people in malevolence; that is, they want them to be less able to defend themselves, or to subvert the entirety of Western civilization through domineering and tyranny. These, however, seem to be a small minority of those making such arguments. We have already stated that advocates of diminishing the militia fall into two basic camps- those who merely want "common sense" gun regulations and those who want a full disarmament. As we have seen before, the latter often are facetious and merely attempting to antagonize a response.

The former is more nuanced- for every person seeking the first steps towards tyranny in a slow manner, seeking to "boil the frog" and eventually disarm much or all of the militia, there are a hundred people who have merely been convinced by decades of propaganda that "common sense reform" is a "good idea." They mean no harm- they have been convinced that society is safer if the population is less well armed. Often, the propaganda employed to elicit such a reaction is the same as that used for other policies- namely, the timeless appeal to "thinking of the children." This is why when maniacs enter an invariably unguarded or poorly guarded school and kill children, the same tired debate rages, the same tired lines are trotted out, and the same impassioned but disturbingly vacuous excuses are made for why school children are not better defended, whether by security forces, or militia, or armed teachers, or even by themselves.

It is utterly foolish to presume that everyone proposing "gun control" is doing so out of malevolence or subversion. There are some who do, and yes, the slogans, the pitiful legal points made, may be similarly debunked and dumb, but that does not make the person proposing them an agent of evil. Mostly, it makes them one who has been fooled by propaganda and subversion themselves. Mostly, these individuals are doing what members of the lawful militia seek to do- to avoid harm, especially to the nation at large and to innocents therein. There is, ironically, therefore, a common ground between the two. While it can be frustrating attempting to educate those who have been fooled, it should be left to people with the stamina and intellect to do so, and others with less patience should perhaps omit themselves from the debate altogether, for fear they will alienate people who out of no fault of their own simply believe lies or half-truths, because they have been spoon-fed them by those who *genuinely are* subversive in manner.

When I speak with someone so clouded in judgment that they think the militia is the national guard, "regulation" includes the government, and the founders only dreamed of people owning muskets, I am bemused, not angered. I do not judge them, because the educational system has been employed in much of the United States to teach the people lies- not just in the realm of constitutional law, but in all other areas as well. My reaction is one of pity and occasional wry humor, not of hatred, dislike, or even annoyance. I suggest this be considered by proponents of the lawful militia as a topic of exceptional import.

XX: STAND YOUR GROUND, CASTLE DOCTRINE, ETC

One subject which is of note in the debate over gun rights does not necessarily need to include firearms, but certainly does on many occasions; namely, the subject of laws regarding self defense.

A number of US states have enshrined what is called "castle doctrine", which considerably lowers the threshold for self defense claims when force is utilized on ones' own property (usually also referring to commercial property and vehicles, not just primary residence.) Another doctrine is called "Stand your Ground"- in which to varying degrees, a person is entitled to use force to defend themselves in situations regardless of where they are, if a person is being substantially aggressive towards them- especially if the defender is cornered and incapable of escaping.

These are common sense laws in clear keeping with the intent of the founders- but proponents of weakening the militia have vilified them, often on the basis of carefully cherry-picked cases where the person who has been attacked is of a certain race or gender. But the founders countenanced the concept of pistol duels, routinely had to defend themselves against raids by hostile "native" forces, and in some US states, being armed if one was male and of voting age was not just a right but considered a legal responsibility. There is not much debate to be had over the ability to defend oneself- with or without a firearm- in ones' own place of residence, and as such these topics are effectively secondary debates of little particular meaning, other than pointing out the fairly clear-cut concept that no founder ever seems to have taken issue with the concept that a person should be able to defend themselves if under reasonable threat of hostility- because they did so on a routine basis.

XXI: REBELLION AS A NON-STARTER FOR ANTIGUN LAWS

Another point sometimes brought up by those who seek to limit the militia is that of rebellion. We have already discussed that the militia is lawful, and that criminal action is not an action of the militia *per se*, and so forth, but in the wake of any politically motivated attack of any kind involving a handgun- whether properly represented or analyzed in a hyperbolic and propagandistic manner (we might look at the riot of January 6th, 2021 for a latter example), efforts at restricting the militia tend to increase, on a few counts:

First, that the founders would hang their heads in shame at the concept of a group of citizens "attempting to subvert Democracy" or something akin.

Second, that further restrictions on firearm ownership are necessary to prevent such actions.

But the founders were well aware of rebellion in their own time and never addressed this by attempting to restrict the actions of the militia. The Whiskey Rebellion occurred under George Washington, and it was the militia which was mustered to suppress it. Prior to the constitution even being crafted, while the United States operated under the Articles of Confederation, Shays Rebellion broke out- again suppressed not by regular troops, but by armed militia commanded by Benjamin Lincoln.

Even in the aftermath of the US Civil War, the only anti-militia rules instituted dealt with the previously mentioned former slave population in relation to Cruikshank. At a time when the nation was nearly torn apart by fighting which cost hundreds of thousands of lives, two generations removed from the nations' founding, we see once again no precedent was created to disarm anyone or to limit their activity as militia members, that was not entirely subjugate to fear and paranoia, and a will to suppress and to abuse members of the population because of their race.

Riots and squabbles occur frequently in most nations; often they involve people disliking some new tax or regulation- our founders (again, including our first president, Washington himself) dealt with such issues not by suppressing the militia, but in *utilizing the militia*. When this is mentioned, it can be expected that the proponent of weakening the same will remark that the militia is an antiquated concept in the age of standing armies- but some of the founders had been involved with crafting the ill-fated Articles of Confederation which actually *explicitly banned* the creation of a standing military force by the federal government, and even by the states save for a few particular situations. While the Articles were abandoned, the basic premise remained; the second amendment was clearly crafted in the wake of the same former standard to maintain an armed populous able to be mustered- a populous which of necessity therefore would need to be able to own and carry their own arms; because otherwise the militia was incapable of functioning. Rebellion never changed the mind of anyone at the time, it seems, for I have tried in vain to find a single example of anyone of note well into the mid 19th century in the United States, proclaiming that the civilian population should be less well armed.

XXII: THE "TIMES HAVE CHANGED" FALLACY

Have the times changed? Yes, in some ways. Firearms have changed since the late 18th century- the average firearm today is considerably more reliable than those present before modern metallurgy, self contained rounds, and smokeless powder.

While it is self evidently irrelevant that the times have changed, we should visit the argument regardless, and look for an effective counter; the claim is actually *not* about guns per se, but is a side argument trotted out at least occasionally by those who seek to undermine the militia. The claim is that the population is troubled by nuisances which did not exist at the same level when the nation was founded; gangs, drug use, and lunacy being the three most common counterparts to the argument.

I laugh heartily when this argument is made. That is because I enjoy studying the history of the 19th century especially as a hobby, partially tied to my work editing old books. Let us take a casual stroll through the period of the late 1700s into the dawn of the 20th century- again, it should be noted, a period in which the only gun laws in the United States were aimed at keeping former slaves and their progeny disarmed.

The history of medicine plays a role here. When we encounter the claim that the modern population is doped up more than those living in the 18th century (and especially the 19th), we can dismiss it almost out of hand- the 18th century ended with the overprescription of opium and other narcotics, and the 19th ended with most of the population using cocaine for toothaches, laudanum for infant colic, and marijuana for effectively any purpose, in tincture form of course- all of those fancy "edible" marijuana snacks sold in some places today are antiquated- the great great grandparents of the consumer are likely to have utilized much the same drug for medicinal reasons.

What of gangs? Highwaymen existed in the late 18th century. Who suppressed them? Often it was *the militia.*

Pirates also existed. Even under the Articles of Confederation, standing forces were permitted to defend against them, but who most often had to fight them? Armed civilians at sea, and in port, again, *the militia.*

Indeed the concept of utilizing a standardized investigative format to determine criminality did not even exist in the late 18th century- This era was only scant on a century parted from the Salem Witch Trials. Justice for significant crimes normally meant being hunted down by armed civilians, for there was seldom any other force of arms to be employed. Gang violence, or at least violence by organized groups in general, prior to the relatively modern period, was generally dealt with by armed locals.

What of lunacy? The founders would not have considered most of todays' "mentally ill" to be lunatics and would have accepted them as members of the militia. We have plenty of writings within the history of medicine to establish what lunatics or "the mad" were in the context of the late 18th and early 19th century- they did not suffer from depression, or "attention deficit disorder", and they were not "on the spectrum"- criminal lunatics; that is, the genuinely mad, were people who were either repetitively violent, murderous, or incapable of understanding basic principles such as right and wrong under the law. These individuals were jailed, put into asylums, or kept at home under their families' care. If the proponents of limiting the militia were pragmatic they would argue for a return of asylums and for a plea to the public to have greater care for troubled relatives and friends, rather than seek to disarm people unrelated to such "lunacy."

XXIII: "THE US MILITARY CAN DESTROY THE MILITIA"

If the US military would ever be successfully utilized to destroy the militia- in direct counter to the US constitution- then the militia must of necessity be well armed and able to resist such a massive tyranny and to stop such an act.

If the US military would not partake in such a venture, the argument is null and void and the lawful militia should do as it pleases, simply because it may, and is granted ability to do so.

I am being deliberately glib; but I will explain in further detail why this is potentially the *single weakest* argument actually made by those who wish to limit or destroy the militia.

First, we may point to the loyalty to the constitution professed by the military. It is not likely that the military could be utilized to destroy a hundred million American lives simply due to this singular factor. Yes, soldiers have been misused by government forces before (notably at Kent State), but these far smaller, more limited incidents are not quite on par with a nation-wide manhunt for every citizen unwilling to subject to tyranny. Even if only one percent of the militia was willing to take up arms against domestic tyranny, we would still be reckoning a force far more large, well armed, and well organized, than some forces which have effectively defeated the US military. Additionally, a portion of the US military would defect and subvert its own ranks.

Second, we may consider those who would simply refuse to fight at all. Another portion of the US military would stand down, not fighting its own, but also categorically refusing to destroy law abiding US citizens.

Third we have the triple quandary: In addition to the

civilian militia and potential defecting US soldiers fighting against such a maneuver, we have three well armed and trained groups which the state would need to grapple with: First; veterans, often with combat experience, and sometimes with a gripe against the state anyways. Second; police forces, especially sheriffs offices which have been exceptionally averse to additions to anti-militia regulation in general. Third; state guard members afforded military training and equipment, that if only for partisan reasons may at least be commanded by state governors not to intervene, or may even side with the dissenting militia.

There is a further complication for the government should it ever choose to try and suppress the militia and its lawful practices; its supply lines would need to stretch across an entire continent and would be indefensible- especially when a significant number of soldiers would be required just to hold down a few of the largest cities and industrial zones in the nation.

It is useless to worry about such a hammer-handed move anyways. Those who support the militia sometimes worry about a sudden middle-of-the-night attack on their right to be militia- I have cautioned before (and will continue to do so) that such a transparent move is massively unlikely in our lifetime; it is much more likely that the slow trickling effect of legalese and marginal social movement will endanger the militia. The points I have made here suffice; tanks cannot guard street corners, and the US military would lose in a fight against the militia unless commanded to utilize nuclear weapons; which would reduce the nation to a crater-pockmarked landscape generally resembling one of the rings of hell from Dante's *Inferno*. Such an attempted decision would like as not be met with mutiny. Arguments which actually bear weight are more reasonable to debate at all.

XXIV: THE MYTH OF "COMMON SENSE GUN CONTROL"

We have already briefly remarked upon the fact that most who seek to denigrate the rights of the militia do not do so from a position of malevolence but rather one of confusion and ignorance. This is important in the sense of debating these issues; but what are the "common sense" laws being proposed? They are all unconstitutional, and they are all also easily rebutted.

First, we have "safe storage" laws. These come in many forms but the overall premise is that to prevent accidental discharge or the use of stolen firearms by criminals, firearms should be safely stored in homes and vehicles, and the onus is on the owner to secure the weapons.

Common sense! At least until pragmatism is examined; if weapons have to be stored when not in explicit use and currently being physically held by the owner, they are far less useful in home defense as the time to deploy them will be greatly increased. Indeed, it would require gun owners to wear their primary weapon on them while asleep. Secondly, the law is either effectively unenforcable, or requires the violation of the fourth amendment routinely, as police will potentially have to randomly check peoples' homes to make sure storage systems are present and in use. Finally, we may point out that only a tiny number of accidental shootings result from the most often proposed reason for the storage laws; namely that children or housemates may accidentally discharge the weapon. The law is therefore a non-starter with only a tiny impact on gun deaths or gun crimes.

Second we have "universal background checks." This is widely supported, and does not, *per se,* violate the rights of the militia in any meaningful sense at all, as background checks are already in full force to begin with- few weapons are sold off the books, and often involve family members or neighbors who can vouch for one another. The premise is pointless because the vast majority of sales *already have such a check*, and almost all sales which do involve criminal intent happen as the result of stolen weapons and the deal takes place in the inner city and involves gang activity. Again; it would be more fruitful to target such gangs and not gun owners who swap with their neighbor down the road.

Third, we have taxes on firearms. This is confusing, since it would only have an impact on the rights of militia members who have less money. By the logic employed by a significant number of people who propose new anti-gun laws at all, that makes the concept both racist and unlawful. Such taxation is already levied on some classes of weapons (such as machine guns and explosive devices) and has a minimal impact (if any) on crime.

Fourth, a ban on "assault weapons." That is, a ban on semi-automatic rifles with certain aesthetic features. This is also a meaningless proposal as such weapons are used in a small minority of gun crimes. Indeed, they are not even disproportionately represented in statistical data regarding the mass shootings (an ambiguous term) usually used as a reason for why such a law needs to exist. The negligible impact such a law would have on gun deaths overall is outweighed by the resulting mass buy-back which would need to be additionally passed into law to requisition the weapons- one which would result in possibly thousands of fatalities, violate the constitution, and in the end fail anyways when a large number of such weapons are reported "missing" before the act could take place. Only lawful members of the militia would be disbarred the use of such arms- criminals would ignore the law as they do all others.

CONCLUSION

I conclude this little work by merely stating that I sincerely desire that this text is helpful in promoting the common welfare and securing the rights of the militia. While I hold the truth to be self evident that a lawful population can only be classed as citizens instead of slaves if generally well armed, and additionally that the population has suffered less abuse foreign and domestic over time by virtue of its nigh on inexhaustible firepower, these are not considered self evident facts by those promoting the denigration of the rights of the citizenry- and as such, incredulity and eye-rolling will get us nowhere. Only a *truly* common sense rebuttal will suffice.

As one final note; it is always worth remembering that the goal of a debate is rarely to convince ones' opponent- it is almost always a delicate linguistic dance performed to win over the (sometimes few) undecided onlookers.

THE END